This Walker book belongs to:

Potato Beetle
Stick Insect
Slug
Praying Mantis
Daddy Long-Legs
Ladybird
Fly
Worm
Cicada
Caterpillar
Dragonfly
Butterfly
Ant
Slug
Potato Beetle
Caterpillar

Rhino Beetle

Butterfly

Grasshopper

Rhino Beetle

Solitary Bee

Ladybird

Katydid

Centipede

Moth

Longhorn Beetle

Spider

Butterfly

For Esther, the bee's knees
K.S.

For Hattie, who loves bugs! Love, Tor xx
T.F.

WALKER BOOKS
AND SUBSIDIARIES
LONDON • BOSTON • SYDNEY • AUCKLAND

First published 2025 by Walker Books Ltd, 87 Vauxhall Walk, London SE11 5HJ

EU Authorized Representative: HackettFlynn Ltd, 36 Cloch Choirneal, Balrothery, Co. Dublin, K32 C942, Ireland. EU@walkerpublishinggroup.com • This book has been typeset in New Century Schoolbook Printed in China • British Library Cataloguing in Publication Data: a catalogue record for this book is available from the British Library • ISBN 978-1-5295-1315-8 • www.walker.co.uk • 10 9 8 7 6 5 4 3 2 1

Kathryn Simmonds
Tor Freeman
Trouble at the Bug Hotel
Solitary bees make their own little nests for one, and the male bees can't sting. All solitary bees love peace and calm!

I'm a solitary bee. The name's Branwell.

When my nest was flattened …
sure, I was a little upset, but anger isn't my style.

People expect me to sting, just because I'm a bee,
and maybe I do look a little scary,
but outsides aren't the same as insides.

The kid just likes colourful things.
I get that. I liked those flowers too.
Still, all this left me with a problem.

I needed a bed…

I needed …

the Bug Hotel.

BUG
HOTEL
BUG
HOTEL

“Room for one, sir?”

The manager was a little snooty.

Some grasshoppers are.

“That’s right, I’m a solitary bee.

The name’s Branwell.”

He showed me to the lift.

I pointed out my wings, but he wasn't impressed.

"Many of our guests can fly, sir.

They come here to relax."

I have to admit, the place was a world away from my usual dirt pile.

Fancy dining room...

Rooftop terrace...

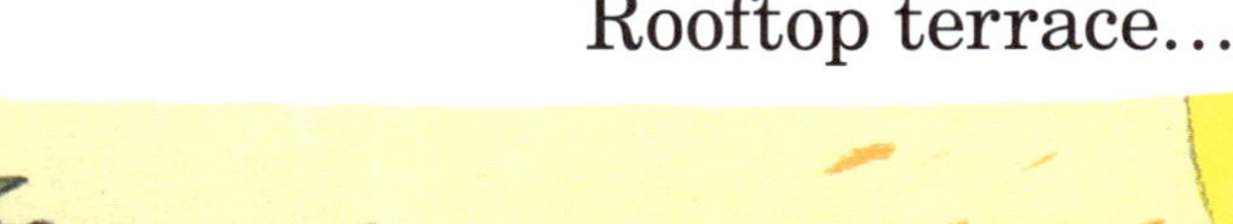

Even a pool, if water is your thing.

"Our guests like to mix and mingle," said the grasshopper.

I sighed. Mixing and mingling had never worked out for me.

That evening I made a special effort, even put on a bow tie.

"Nectar, please. Make it a large one."

The nectar was sweet, but the whispering had already begun.

"Look out, Clarice. There's a bee amongst us!"

"Don't sit there, Gordy. He might sting!"

Same old, same old.

What did they take me for – a wasp?
"Solitary bees don't sting," I muttered.
But nobody was listening.

At least there was a cabaret show.
Butterflies always lift my mood.

On my way out, I passed the grasshopper.

"Enjoying your stay, sir?"

"A little trouble with the mingling," I said.

"I imagine it's because sir is a bee."

"Solitary bees don't sting!" I pointed out,

but he'd already hopped off.

I ate alone.

So they didn't like me?

Well, they didn't even know me.

Suddenly …

WHAAAA - WHA
WHAAA - WHAAA

an almighty noise rang out.

Then a voice – the grasshopper's:

"All guests to the dining room *immediately*!"

He sounded scared.

A daddy long-legs was trembling the way only a daddy long-legs can.

"What's the problem?" I asked.

"It's the Kevin Alarm!" he replied, real wobbly.

"The *what* alarm?" I said.

"Kevin, young, human, utterly fearless? He's heading for the hotel!" said the long-legs in a whispery voice.

So that was Kevin!

The kid who squashed my nest. He sure had some energy.

First came the shaking.

Then the prodding.

And finally …

the grabbing.

"Felicity!" cried a centipede.

"Worm!" cried Kevin.

"That's not a worm; that's my wife!" the centipede wailed.

"He's got Errol, too!" shouted a beetle. "He's trying to..."

Yup, the kid was trying to eat him.

"MERCY!" shrieked Errol.

But Kevin knew no mercy. He only knew curiosity.

In went a leg. In went a wing.

Luckily for Errol, he tasted disgusting.

Now it was Felicity's turn. What a scene!

Everyone lost it. Especially the grasshopper.

"We're doomed!" he cried. "Where's the bee?

BRANWELL, USE YOUR STING!"

The others joined in:

"STING HIM, BRANWELL!

STING HIM!"

I'd had just about enough.

"Please listen. I don't sting, and I don't *want* to sting, so let's cut the screaming!"

They kept right on screaming.

What did the kid like? Of course … colour!

"I hate to ask," I said to the butterflies,
"because this could be dangerous…"

The brightest one answered: "We may be delicate
but we can still be brave."

"Like you say, outsides aren't the same as insides,"
added another.
So I told them my plan, and they listened.

I counted them in:
"Three...
Two...
One..."

Swoosh!!!

I'm telling you, that little kid had never seen anything like it.

He spun.

He gasped.

He giggled.

And in no time, Kevin forgot all about the bug hotel and followed those dazzling butterflies back up the garden.

So that's how we saved the Bug Hotel.
And nobody had to get stung. I told you, I'm not that kind of bee.
The manager said I could stay as long as I wanted.
He even gave me the VIB room (that's Very Important Bee).

The other guests are a whole lot friendlier now, too.
Turns out, once they got to know me,
they couldn't get enough of me.

And as for eating alone?

Let's just say …

these days, I'm not such a solitary bee.

Potato Beetle
Stick Insect
Slug
Praying Mantis
Daddy Long-Legs
Ladybird
Fly
Worm
Cicada
Caterpillar
Butterfly
Dragonfly
Ant
Slug
Potato Beetle
Caterpillar

Rhino Beetle

Butterfly

Grasshopper

Rhino Beetle

Ladybird

Solitary Bee

Katydid

Centipede

Moth

Longhorn Beetle

Spider

Butterfly

Kathryn Simmonds writes fiction, poetry and picture books. Her poetry collection *Sunday at the Skin Launderette* won the Forward Prize for Best First Collection and was shortlisted for the Costa Poetry Prize. She also writes short stories, which have been published in magazines and broadcast on BBC Radio. Her first picture book was *Be My Sunflower*, illustrated by Rosalind Beardshaw. Kathryn lives in Norwich, and her favourite bug is a dragonfly.

Tor Freeman is one of only a handful of artists to have been granted the prestigious Sendak Fellowship. With author Michelle Robinson, she won the Lollies Prize for *Ten Fat Sausages*. Tor is also the illustrator of Richard Ayoade's *The Book That No One Wanted to Read*, and she has created numerous comics, including *Welcome to Oddleigh*, *Sister Clawdetta*, and many picture books, including the Olive series. Tor lives in London, and her favourite bug is any hairy caterpillar.